Is Santa Real?

"The giver of every good and perfect gift has called upon us to mimic His giving, by grace, through faith, and this is not of ourselves."
                                                        -St. Nicholas

Is Santa Real?
How Saint Nicholas Became Santa

Written by
Jackie Jamison

For Tucker, Molly and Emily.

Illustrations are based on photographs licensed from Dreamstime, and public domain images. Full details are listed at the end of the book.

Copyright © 2016, Jackie Jamison
All Rights Reserved

Are you ready to know the real truth?

A truth, once you know, is always going to be known.

The very sound of Santa Claus' name has magic in it: overflowing stockings, a tree full of presents, and a season of celebration. Santa Claus delights the heart and makes it hard to sleep on Christmas Eve.

Of course many people dress up as Santa around the holidays, but no one sees the real Santa Claus. We imagine him as a jolly, round old man dressed in red that rides in a sleigh and sneaks down chimneys, keeping track of who is naughty and nice.

But is Santa Claus real? Maybe you have wondered how one man can reach all the children of the world in one night? Or deliver presents to the houses without chimneys? Or why he brings some of your friends one present while others five and others ten?

Santa Claus is real. But now that you are old enough, you should know that he is not quite who you thought he was. Santa Claus is a man who lived long ago in a far-off country in the East. This man was named Nicholas, and he loved God and other people so much that he was given the special title Saint. Saint Nicholas was the name everyone originally called Santa.

Nicholas was born just 300 years after Jesus was alive. His mom and dad were rich and noble but they had no children. They prayed and prayed for many years for a child, and when God finally answered their prayers with little Nicholas, the first thing they did was dedicate him to God.

Nicholas' parents loved him very much, but they died from a terrible sickness that swept through the country when he was a teenager. Nicholas inherited all of his parents' great wealth, but instead of being content with his riches, Nicholas devoted himself to God.

Today, if you do not have enough to eat, there are places to go where food is free and there are warm beds on cold nights. A long time ago, people without enough to eat did not have these things. Nicholas cared about the poor and began to give away his riches to help the people who needed it. Nicholas vowed to use all of his wealth to help other people in the name of God.

There lived in Nicholas' town a man of great wealth who had recently lost all of his money. Even worse, the nobleman had never worked, and had no way to make money. The man had three beautiful daughters. When the family began to run out of food, the father became desperate. The only way they could survive, he decided, was if he sold his daughters into slavery.

The father tried to find other options, but he could not. At last the day came when the father told the eldest daughter that tomorrow he would sell her as a slave. Nicholas was passing by on the street and through the open window, he heard the father's desperation and his evil plan. He saw the eldest daughter silently praying, and his heart was filled with compassion.

Nicholas knew that the father was a proud man and would not accept his money, so he began to think how to help. He remembered Jesus' words, not to give your gifts for men to see, but to give in secret where only God can see. Nicholas wanted God to receive all the glory for saving the man's daughters so Nicholas went to their house in middle of the night and threw a bag of gold in through the window.

When the family woke the next morning and discovered the pouch of gold sitting in front of the fireplace, they rejoiced. Instead of selling the eldest daughter into slavery, the father had enough money for her marriage to a respectable man in the town. (In those days a young woman needed a dowry to get married, which was enough money to set up a new household.)

Nicholas saw the father give glory to God because of this gift from heaven, and what good Nicholas' gift had done for the eldest daughter. Nicholas decided that the other girls should have money for marriage as well.

Once again Nicholas crept to the house in the middle of the night and threw in a bag of gold coins, which landed in front of the fireplace. When the father and daughters woke and discovered the gold again, they gave thanks to God. Now the second daughter could be married to a respectable man of the town.

The father knew that gold does not usually fall from heaven. He wondered who was responsible for these gifts, and whether a third mysterious bag of gold would find its way to his fireplace that night for his youngest daughter. He decided that he would stay up to watch, and hid himself in the corner.

Sure enough, near midnight Nicholas came underneath the family's window and threw in a bag of gold. This time the bag landed inside one of the stockings that the youngest daughter had washed that evening and was drying by the fire.

The father ran outside to find who was responsible. He was too fast for Nicholas and caught him by his coat. The father fell to the ground, kissing Nicholas' feet and thanking him. Nicholas told the man to thank God, not himself, and to keep his identity a secret.

Nicholas continued to help the poor in the name of God. He became a priest and then the Bishop of the little town and was widely respected for his love of God and good deeds. When he died, he was honored as a saint for the way he had lived his life for God.

To honor St. Nicholas after his death, every year on a certain day children would leave their shoes or their stockings (what we now call socks) by the fireplace to be filled with good things.

St. Nicholas' special day (December 6th) is near Christmas. As the centuries went on, many people stopped celebrating saints' days. But they did not want to stop honoring St. Nicholas. Many people already exchanged gifts at Christmas in memory of the wise men's gifts to Jesus, and it only made sense to celebrate Nicholas' good gifts for the glory of God on this day as well.

As more people went to churches with pastors instead of priests, they no longer knew what a Bishop would wear. Instead of Nicholas' shiny red Bishop's clothes and pointed hat, people imagined him in a red fur suit.

> Saint --> Santa
> Nicholas --> 'Cholas --> Claus

As some people stopped going to churches that talked about saints, St. Nicholas seemed like an odd, old-fashioned name. Instead of Saint they called him Santa (which means saint in Spanish) and Nicholas was shortened to Claus.

So now you know. Santa Claus is real—he is a man named St. Nicholas, who lived long ago who has changed the world because of the secret presents he gave to the young at night which fell into their stockings hung by the fire.

You can see, of course, that there are other parts of the story of Santa Claus that is told today that are not real. Elves, a magic sleigh, flying reindeer, naughty and nice lists, and a North Pole toy workshop—these are the creation of a world full of people who love Santa Claus, and what he stands for: a world that is fair, exciting, fun and generous.

Because St. Nicholas died hundreds of years ago, he is not the one putting toys into your stocking this Christmas Eve. The people who do that are people who love you and want you to thank God not them for the presents. They are people who want you to know that the most real things in the world are sometimes things you cannot see.

A legend is a story told with love meant to teach something true, even if some of its parts are larger than real life. Have you ever told a story and added details to make it more exciting? That is how the story of St. Nicholas became the legend of Santa Claus. And while the legend of Santa Claus has some parts that are larger than life, we tell it again and again because it reminds us that goodness and joy are real, and that generosity and hope win in the end.

Now you too are a keeper of the story of St. Nicholas and the legend of Santa Claus. Just as your eyes sparkled every year on Christmas Eve waiting for the man in red, now you too can be part of passing on the gifts of love, joy, goodness, and generosity this Christmas.

Illustration Credits

The following illustrations in this book are based on the following licensed photographs from Dreamstime.com:

Page 1 - 61554115 © Yarruta
Page 2 - 60524291© Konstantin Yuganov
Page 3 - 62653929 © Igor Mojzes
Page 4 - 60528091© Konstantin Yuganov
Page 5 - 44107513© Jorisvo
Page 6 - 39165190© Alekuwka
Page 7 - 20522806 © Gerard Koudenburg
Page 8 - 63225078 © Petr Tkachev
Page 9 - 60383752 © Roberto Maggioni
Pages 9, 15, 17 - 63147164 © Floriano Rescigno
Page 10 - 27863334 © Nejron
Page 11 - 65174708 © Grytsaj
Pages 12,15,16 - 16248294 © Evgeniy Kuzmin
Page 13 - 18979939 © Photowitch
Page 14 - 131944 © Dana Rothstein
Page 18 - 47784134 © Wojphoto
  44107490 © Jorisvo
Page 19 - 25998612 © Unholyvault
Page 20 - 32749179 © Mk74
Page 21 - 32651515 © Tmcphotos
  40849347 © Ievgen Melamud
Page 23 - 43875872 © Hans Slegers
Page 25 - 46999597 © Mtlapcevic
Page 26 - 34414526 © Dmitriy Shironosov
Page 27 - 62192327 © Wavebreakmedia Ltd
Border Art - 39432292 © Maaridi
Cover Art - 34414526 © Dmitriy Shironosov
Half Title Page - 46847398 © Dzhamilia Ermakova
Back of Half Title Page - 16174209 © Fotofermer
Title Page - 60926107 © Aleksey Satyrenko

Page 24 – Based on an illustration from The Night Before Christmas and Other Popular Stories For Children. Various Authors. Chicago: W. B. Conkey Company, 1903. Project Gutenberg. Web. February 1, 2016.

Author Note

Thank you for joining me in learning about St. Nicholas and Santa Claus.

Now that you are a keeper of the story of St. Nicholas, how are you going to pass on the gifts of love, joy, goodness, and generosity this Christmas?

Contact me at jackiejamisonwriter@gmail.com or visit my website: www.jackiejamison.com and let me know!

If you have a minute to spare, I would very much appreciate a review on Amazon. Your help in spreading the word is invaluable.

*Link to my Amazon page: http://www.amazon.com/-/e/B01M171FZZ

Thank you!

Jackie Jamison

Made in the USA
Las Vegas, NV
10 December 2024